Handwriting Practice
3rd Grade
Children's Reading & Writing Education Books

PROFESSOR GUSTO
EDUCATIONAL & INFORMATIVE BOOKS FOR CHILDREN
(PRE-K / K-12)

high

high   high   high

high high high

near

near near near

near near near

west

west west west

west west west

best

best best best

best best best

next

next next next

next next next

else

else   else   else

else   else   else

area

area area area

area area area

wife

wife   wife   wife

wife   wife   wife

own

own own own

own own own

base

base base base

base base base

slip

slip   slip   slip

slip   *slip*   *slip*

took

took took took

took took took

yard

yard yard yard

yard yard yard

save

save   save   save

save save save

keep

keep   keep   keep

keep   keep   keep

safe

safe   safe   safe

safe   *safe*   *safe*

easy

easy   easy   easy

easy easy easy

fuel

fuel   fuel   fuel

fuel fuel fuel

iron

iron   iron   iron

iron   iron   iron

city

city   city   city

city   *city*   *city*

hope

hope hope hope

hope hope hope

sign

sign   sign   sign

sign   sign   sign

tiny

tiny   tiny   tiny

tiny   tiny   tiny

hold

hold   hold   hold

hold hold hold

gun

gun   gun   gun

gun   *gun*   *gun*

east

east east east

east east east

sum

sum   sum   sum

sum   sum   sum

milk

milk   milk   milk

milk milk milk

knot

knot knot knot

knot knot knot

wild

wild   wild   wild

wild wild wild

knee

knee knee knee

knee knee knee

seem

seem seem seem

seem seem seem

lady

lady lady lady

lady lady lady

sea

sea sea sea

sea sea sea

open

open open open

open open open

both

both both both

both both both

fact

fact   fact   fact

fact   *fact*   *fact*

Made in the USA
Middletown, DE
30 March 2020

87521859R00024